Kate goes to a farm

Story by Jenny Giles

Illustrations by Sharyn Madder

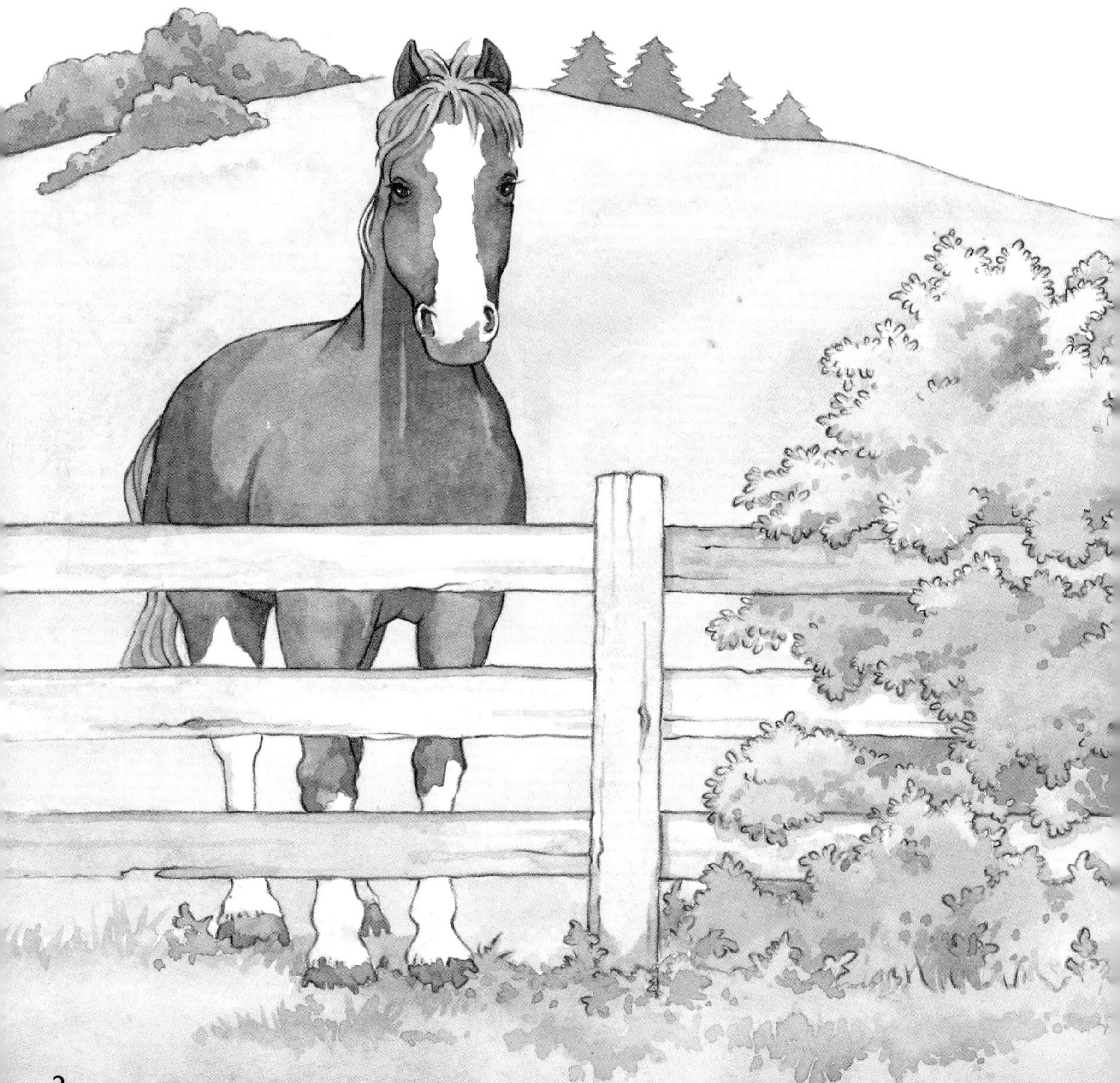

Kate is at a farm.

Dad is at the farm, too.

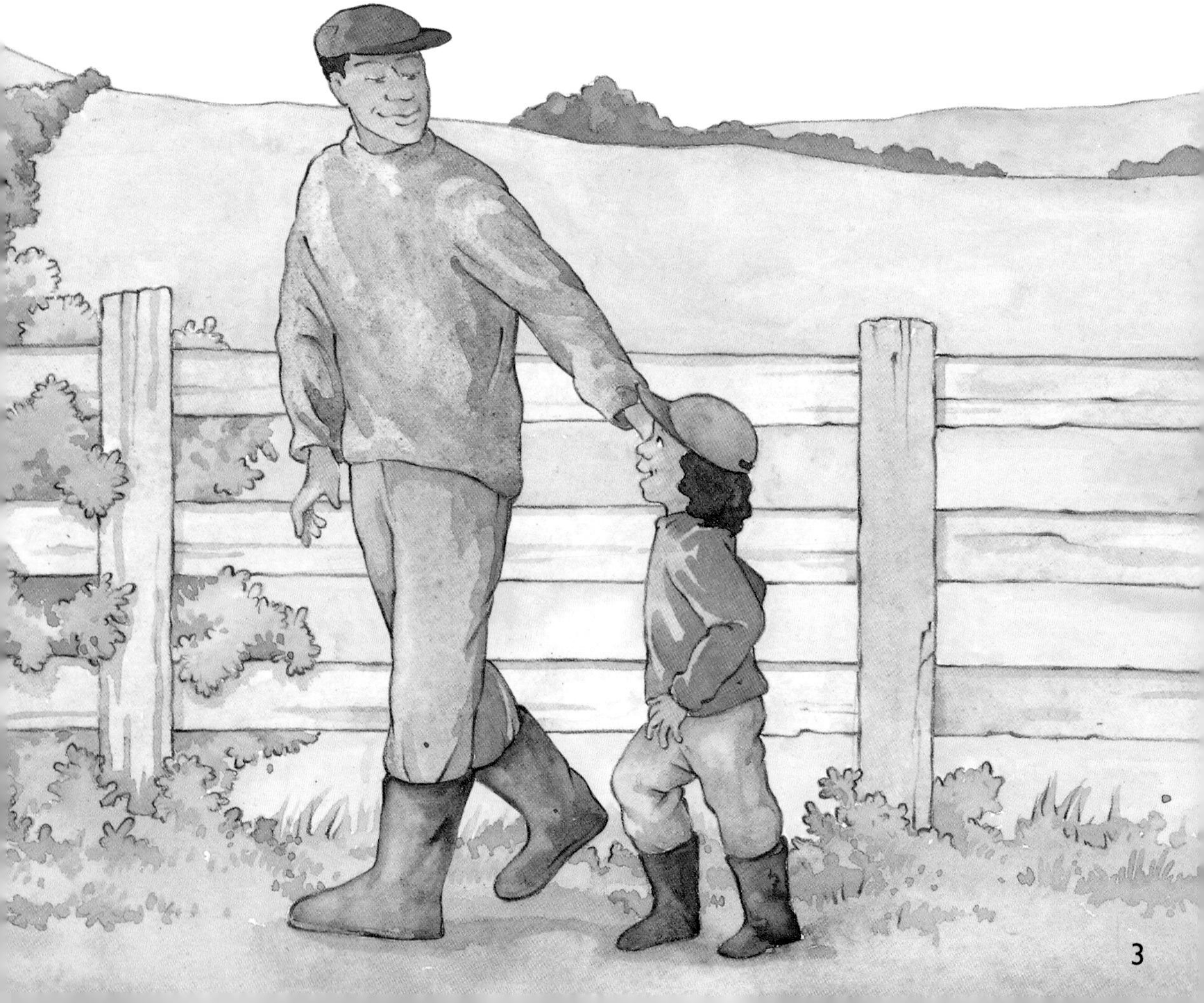

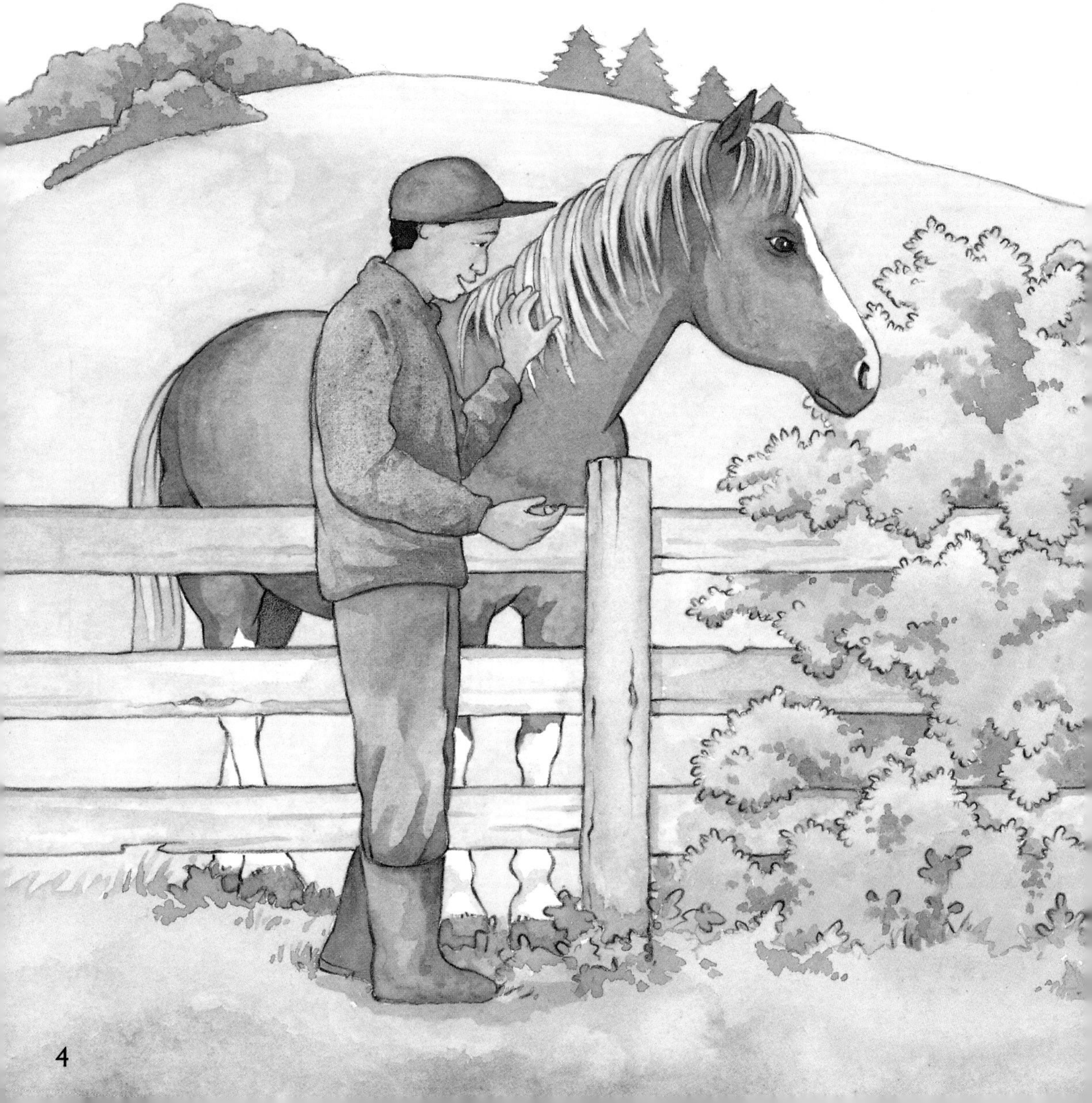

Dad said,

"Come here, Kate.

Look at the horse."

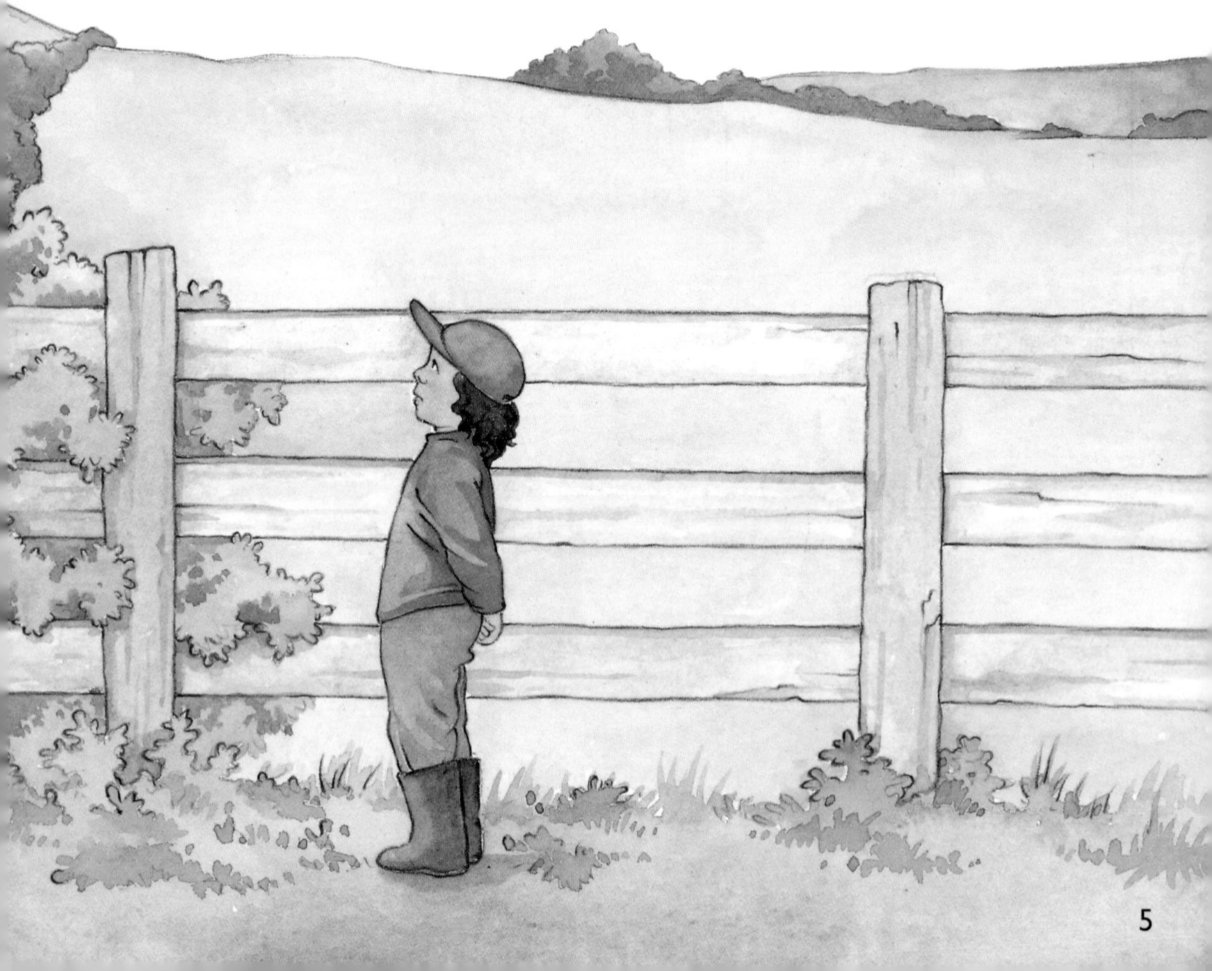

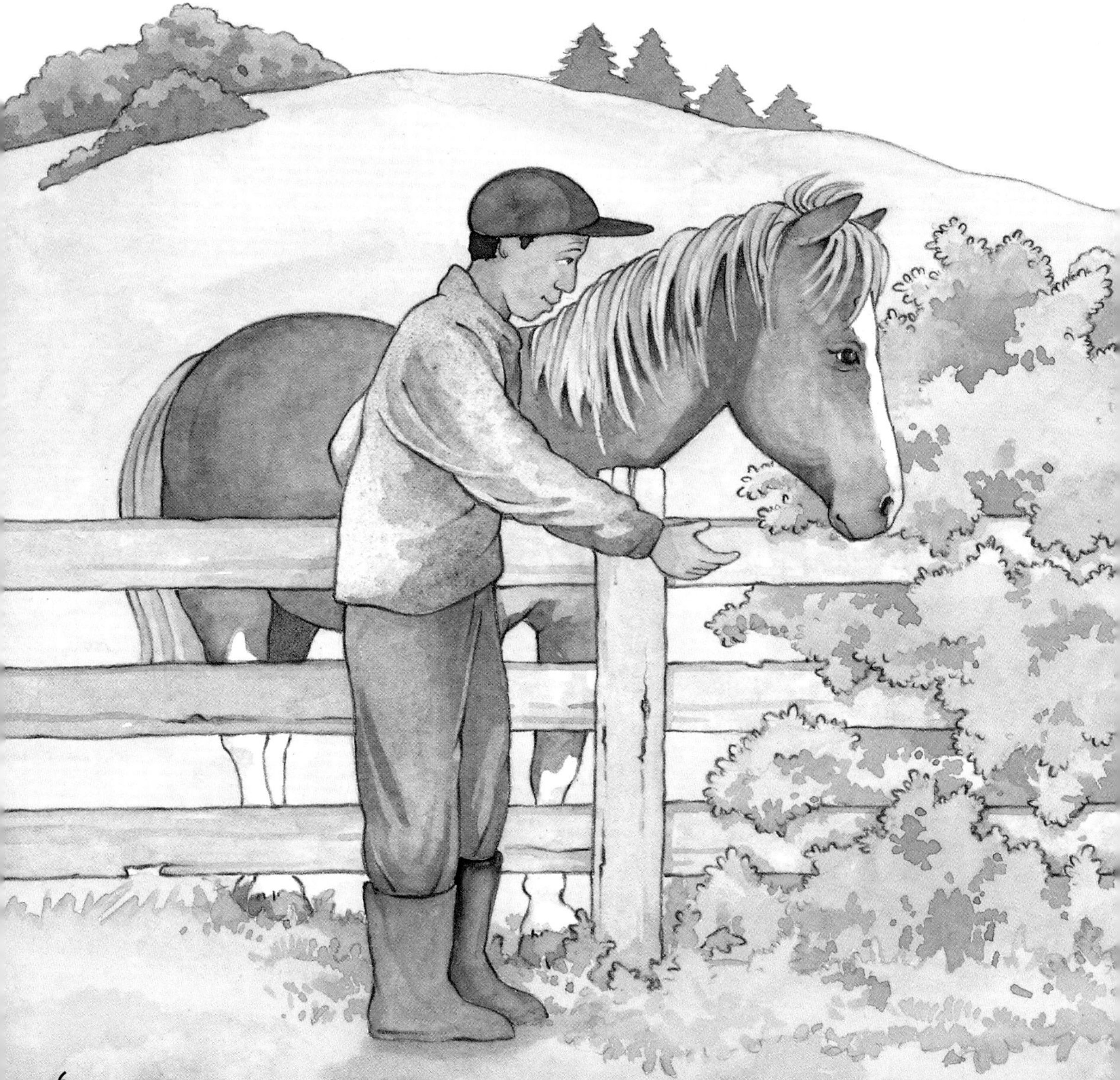

"No," said Kate.

"The horse is too big!"

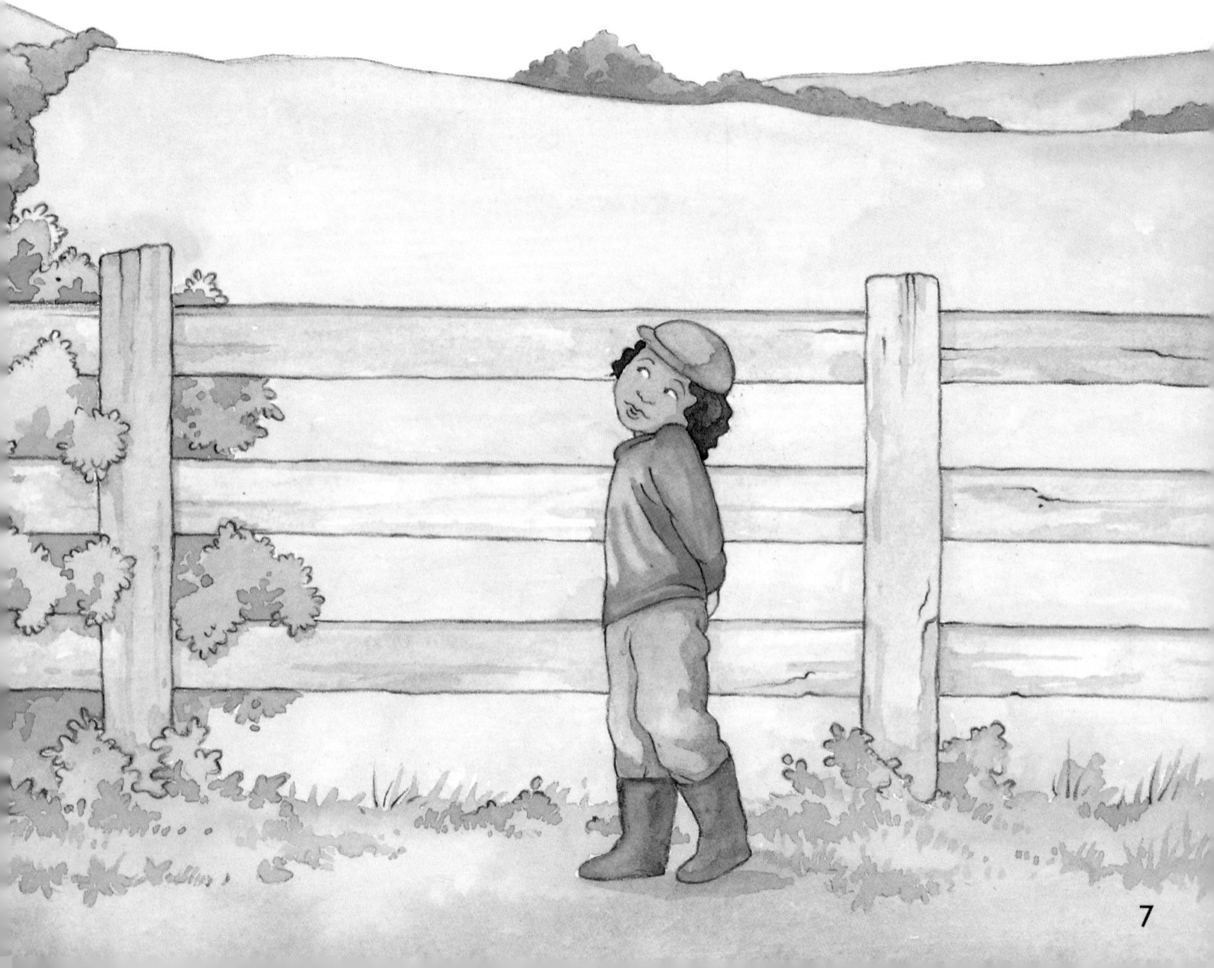

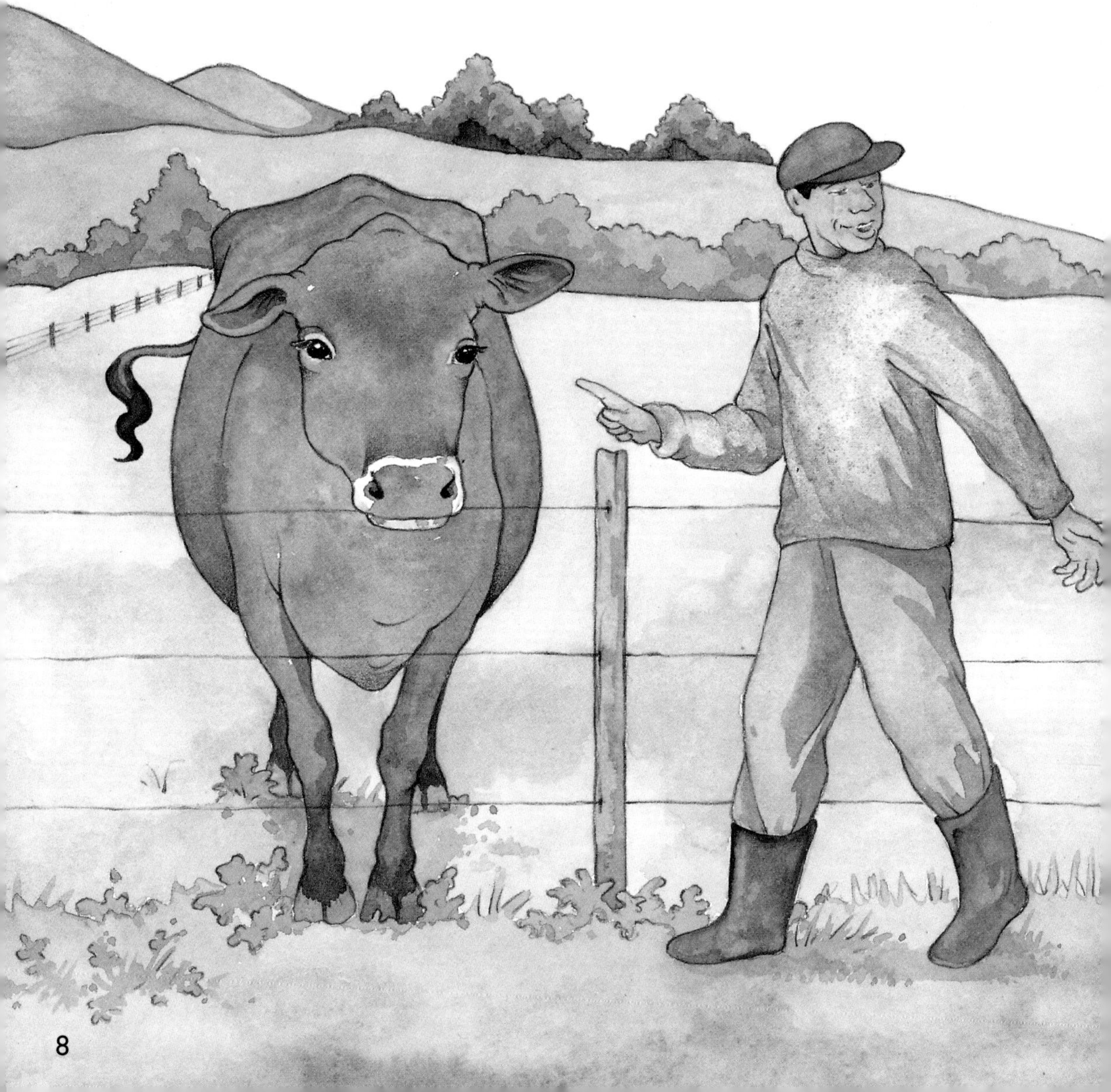

"Come here, Kate," said Dad.

"Here is a cow."

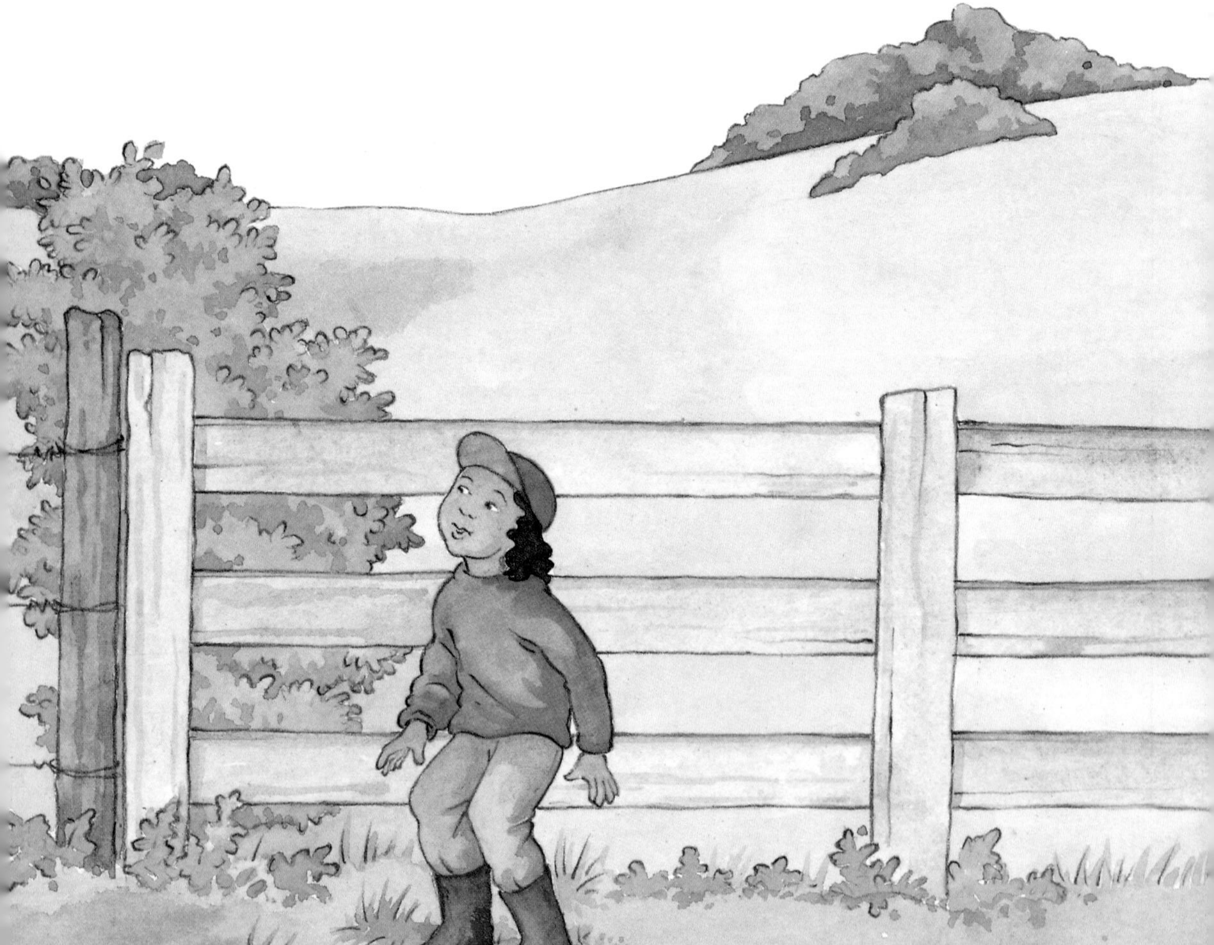

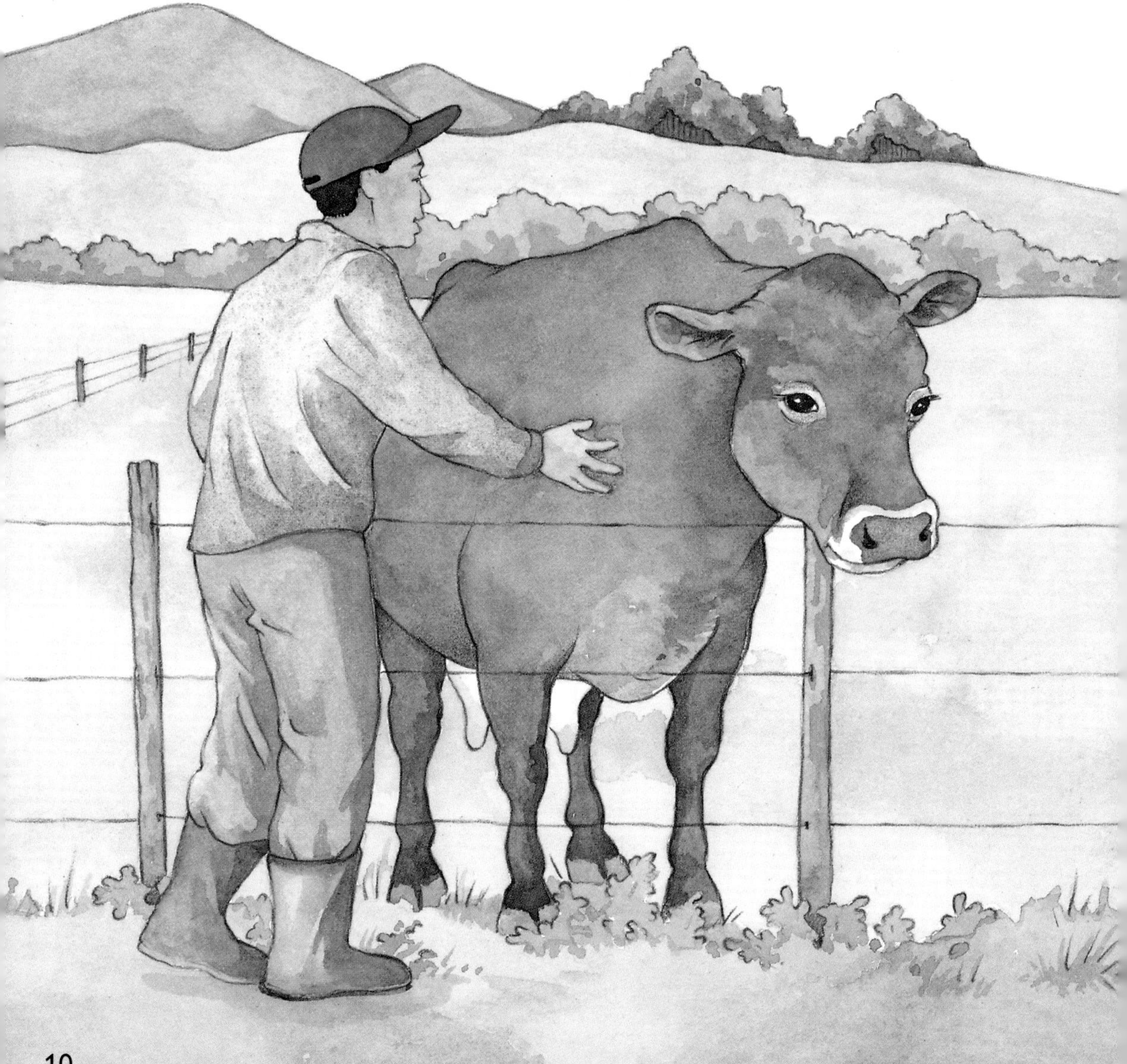

"Come on, Kate," said Dad.

"No," said Kate.

"The cow is too big!"

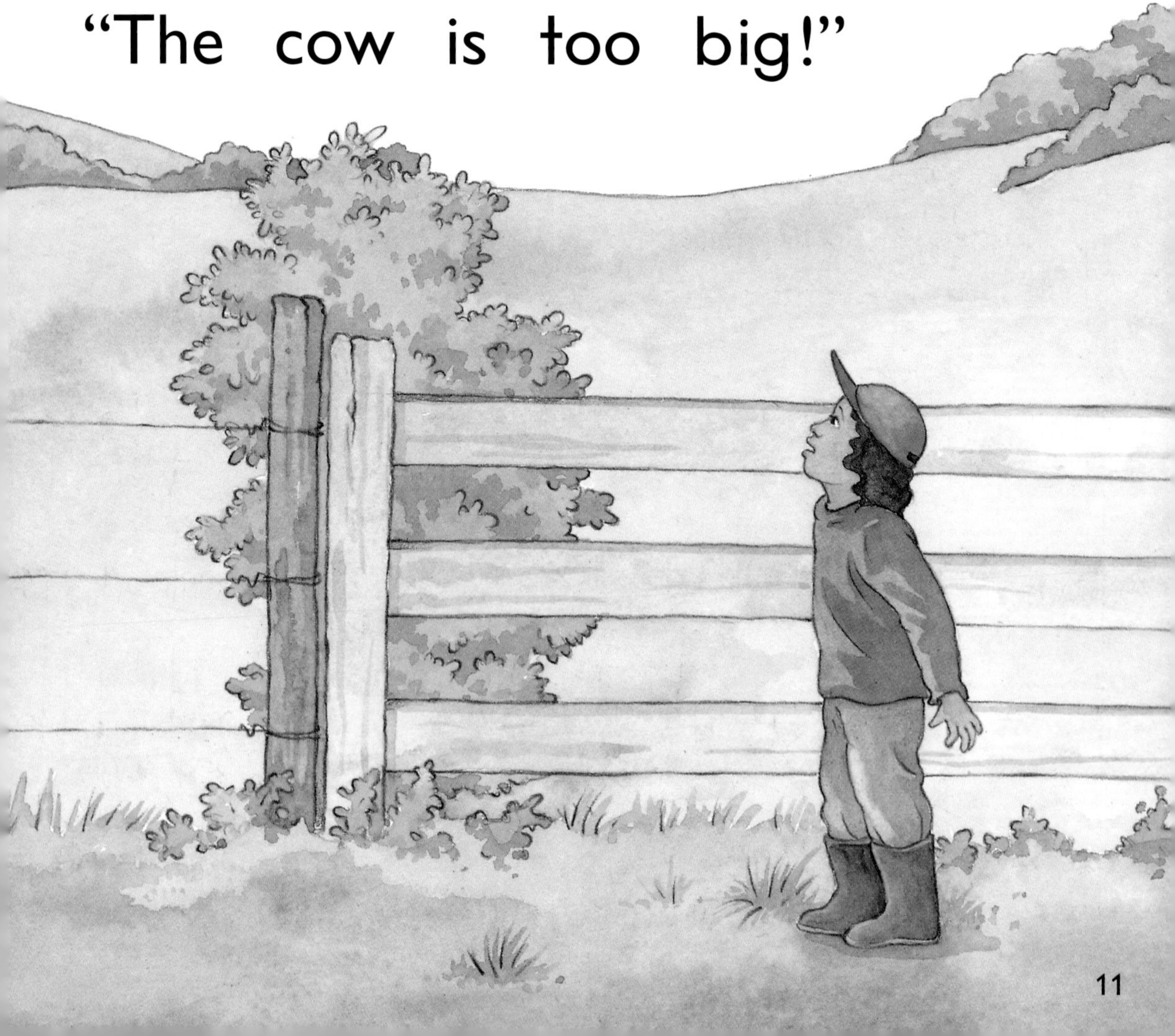

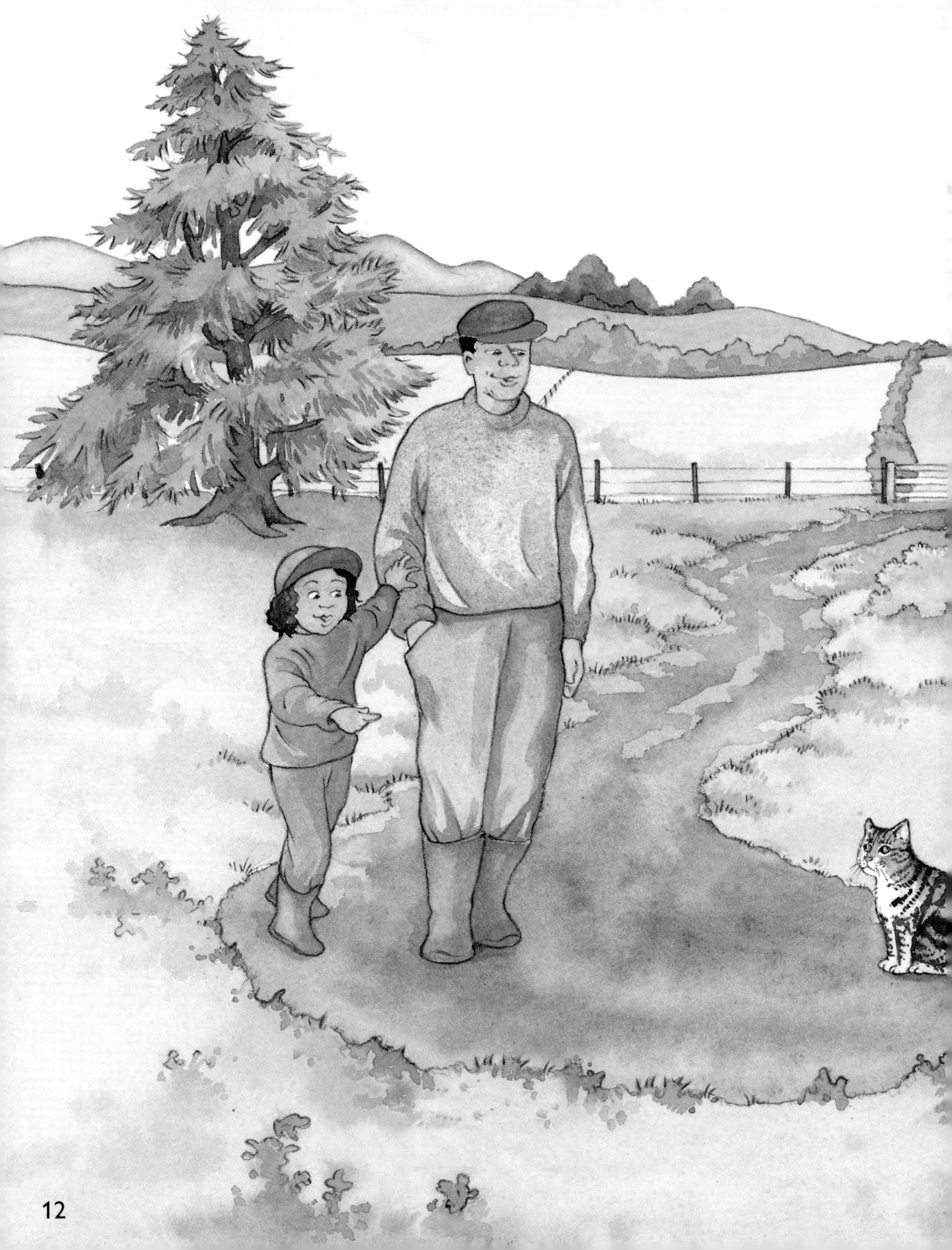

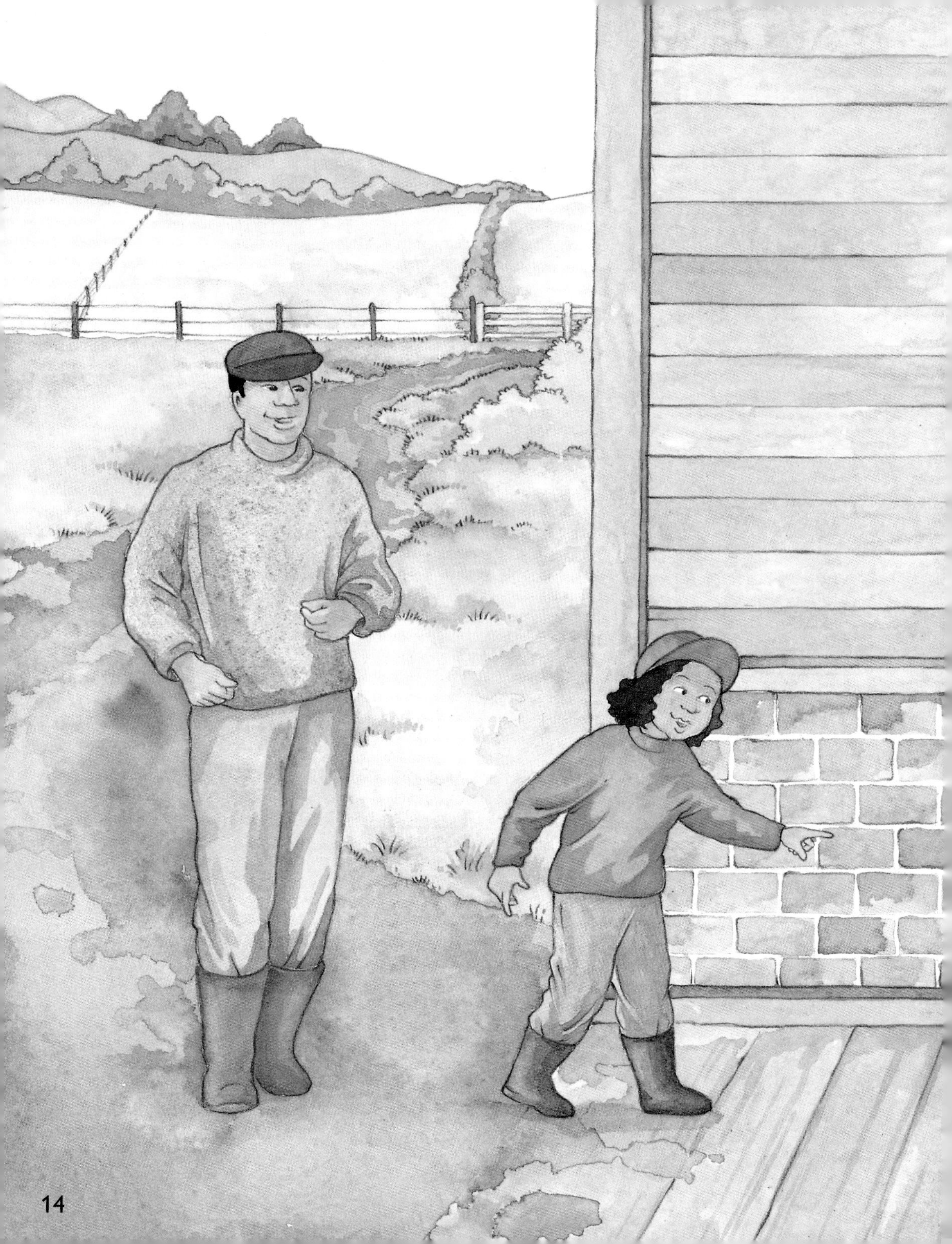

"Look at the **little** kittens!"

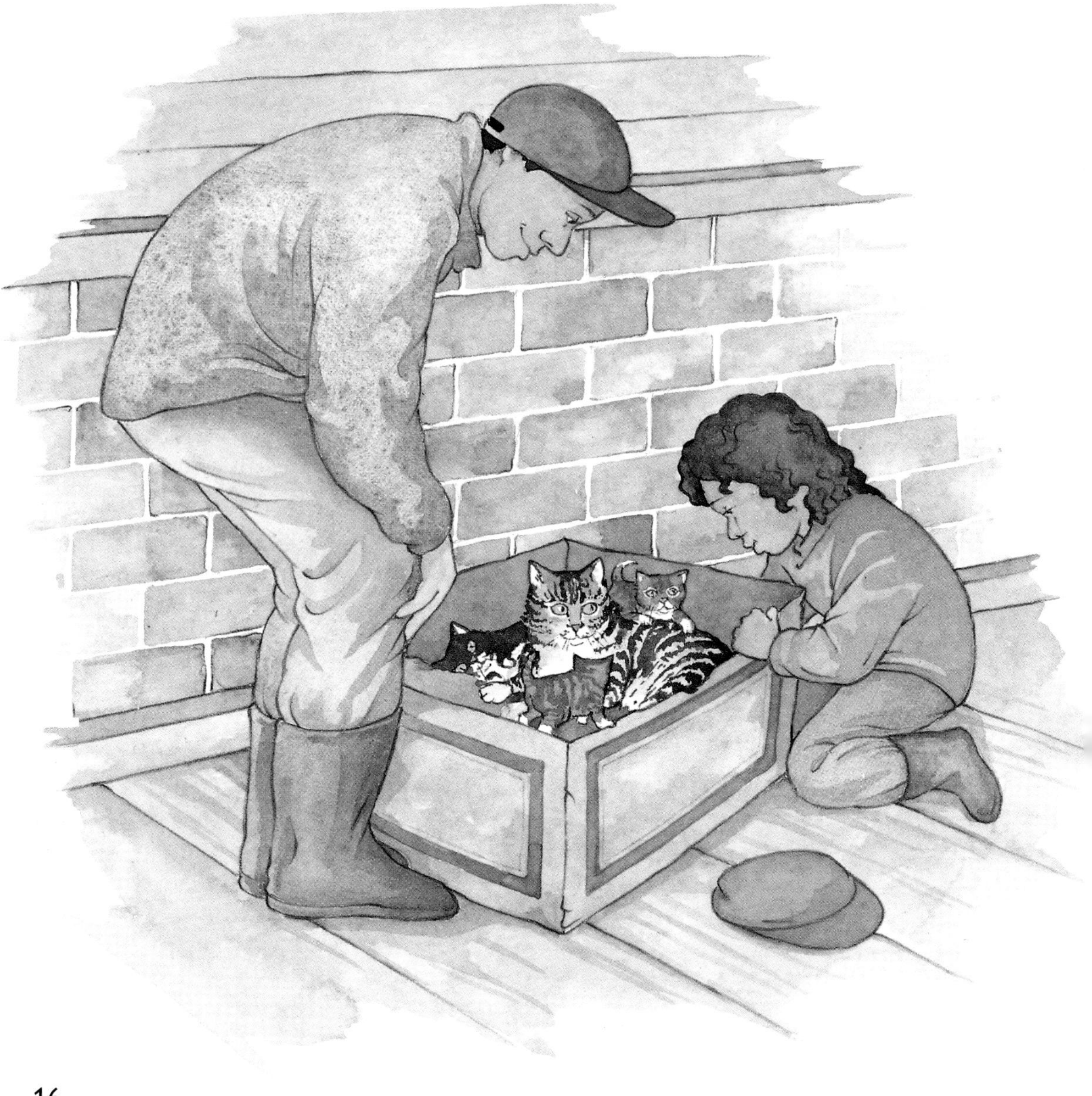

"Come here, Dad,"

said Kate.

"Look!"

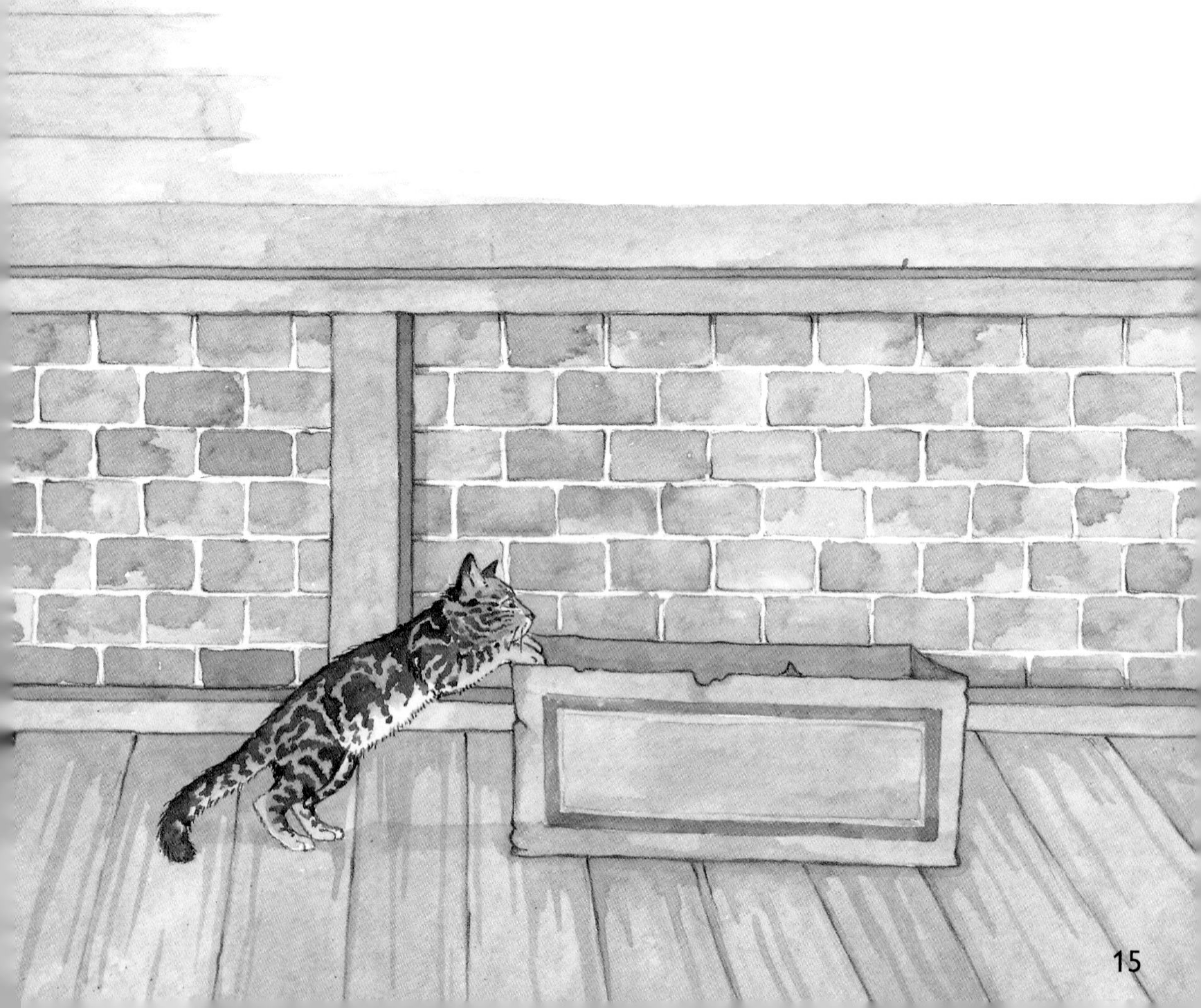

"Look, Dad," said Kate.

"Here is a cat."

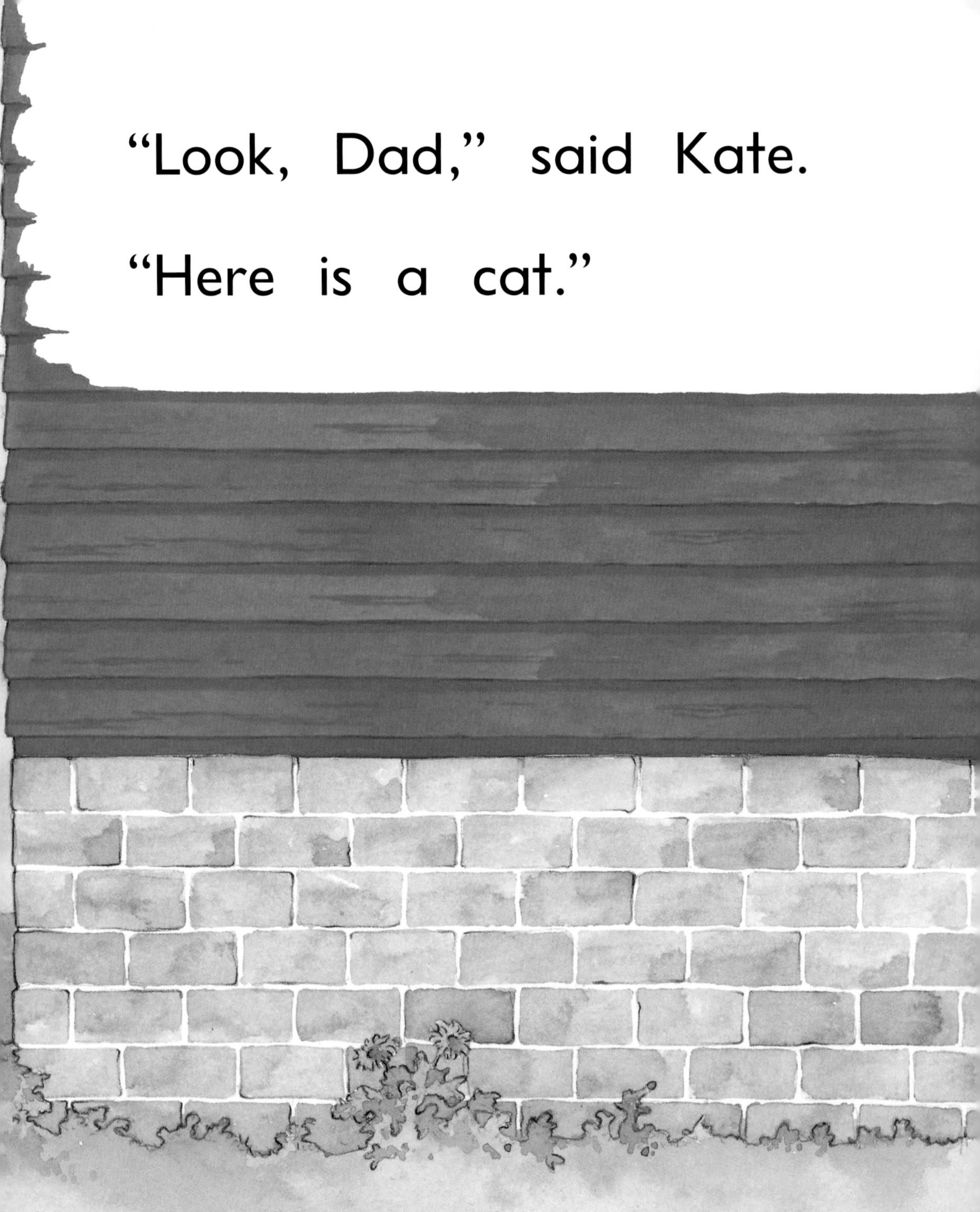